MEDIEVAL TIMES
Activity Book

Author	Linda Milliken
Editor	Deneen Celecia
Designer	Wendy Loreen
Illustrator	Barb Lorseyedi

© 1995 **EDUPRESS** • P.O. Box 883 • Dana Point, CA 92629

ISBN 1-56472-049-7

Table of Contents

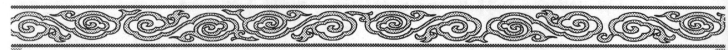

Literature List

- **Castles**
by Beth Smith; Watts LB 1988. (5-7)
Castle history and construction are explained with details on how they changed.

- **Walter Dragun's Town:**
  Crafts and Trade in the Middle Ages
by Sheila Sancha; Harper LB 1988. (5-7)
Reconstruction of the life of artisans and tradespeople in 13th century England.

- **Medieval Cathedral**
by Fiona Macdonald; Bedrick 1991. (3-6)
Explains how cathedrals were built and the role they played in medieval life.

- **Knight**
by Christopher Gravett; Eyewitness Books 1993. (4-7)
Traces the history of knighthood from the 9th to the 17th century.

- **Fourteenth-Century Towns**
by John D. Clare; Harcourt 1993. (3-6)
Life in a medieval town is portrayed with illustrations and text.

- **Life in a Medieval Village**
by Gwyneth Morgan; Harper 1991. (5-7)
A story of activities in a medieval village and the effects of the church on medieval life.

- **The Legend of King Arthur**
by Alan Baker; Doubleday 1990. (4-6)
Merlin narrates the story of Arthur from his birth at Tintagel to his death.

- **A Medieval Feast**
by Aliki; Harper LB 1983. (3-6)
A visit from the king provides the occasion for a well-described feast.

- **Merlin Dreams**
by Alan Lee; Delacorte 1988. (4-6)
Nine enchanting medieval tales from the mind of a dreaming Merlin.

- **Nicobobinus**
by Terry Jones; Bedrick 1986. (5-7)
A medieval boy and his friend go to the Land of the Dragons to seek a cure for his foot.

- **A Connecticut Yankee**
  in King Arthur's Court
by Mark Twain; Morrow 1988. (5-7)
Story of an American who travels through time to Arthurian England.

- **Sir Gawain and the Loathly Lady**
by Selina Taylor, reteller; Lothrop 1987. (5-7)
Sir Gawain honors a pledge and breaks a spell to release a beautiful woman.

- **Illuminations**
by Jonathan Hunt; Macmillan 1989. (3-4)
Illuminated letters of the alphabet introduce different aspects of medieval life.

- **Castles**
by Rachel Wright; Watts LB 1992. (3-6)
Explore the history of castles with projects such as building a castle or making a tapestry.

- **Knights**
by Rachel Wright; Watts LB 1992 (3-6)
Make stained glass windows and a castle with easy-to-find materials.

- **Looking into the Middle Ages**
by Huck Scarry; Harper 1985. (4-6)
A pop-up book that illustrates castles, cathedrals and jousting tournaments.

Medieval Times

Historical Aid

Medieval times, also known historically as the Middle Ages, is the name given to the period in western Europe from the end of the Holy Roman Empire, about 400 A.D., to the beginning of the Renaissance in 1500 A.D.

Churches and Cathedrals

The Christian church dominated the lives and provided leadership for everyone in the early Middle Ages. Popes, bishops and other leaders of the church took over many functions of government after the Roman emperors lost power. The younger sons of noble families often entered the priesthood and were able to collect taxes, called *tithes*, from the villagers. The church also maintained courts of law.

Two church institutions, the cathedral and the monastery, became centers of learning. The monks of some monasteries and the clergy of the cathedrals helped continue the reading and writing of Latin and preserved many valuable ancient manuscripts. They also established most of the schools in Europe.

Lords and Manors

By the 800s most of western Europe was divided into large estates called *manors*. Most of western Europe was united under one ruler, the most influential of which was Charlemagne. A few wealthy landowners, called *lords*, ruled the manors, but most of the people were poor peasants who worked the land. Life was short and difficult. Most people never reached the age of thirty. War, famines and epidemics such as the Black Death killed many.

The Coming of Castles

After the end of Charlemagne's rule, Europe was again divided into many kingdoms. Most of the kings were weak and had little control over their kingdoms. There was constant warfare. Homes became fortresses where inhabitants could defend themselves against the ongoing struggle for more land. These fortified homes, known as *castles* were strategically built to provide protection for a lord and those who served him. A castle became the center of medieval life.

Knights and Knighthood

The Age of the Knight began in about 900 AD. New inventions such as the stirrup and horseshoe turned a horseman into a fighting force. Kings needed knights for fighting, but could not maintain their cost in peacetime so instead of paying wages, some kings agreed to give part of their land in exchange for services, mostly military. This arrangement of land for services was called *feudalism*. Any man granted land was called a *vassal*. A lord and a vassal had rights and duties toward each other. A lord promised his vassal protection and justice. Vassals tithed ten percent of all goods to the lord. Vassals who became knights also arranged with lesser classes to work their land.

In addition to working the fields, peasants protected and cared for livestock, cultivated new land and worked in the vineyards and gardens of the lord. Peasants were very poor. Large families commonly lived together in one-room huts they shared with farm animals.

Growth of Towns

After the 1000s many capable lords provided strong governments and periods of peace. Merchants again traveled the land routes. Towns sprang up along the main trade routes. Most early towns developed near a fortified castle, church or monastery where merchants could stop for protection.

Peasants began to leave the fields and settle into towns where they sought work and developed crafts and the means to earning a living independent of the feudal system. Craftsmen banded together in groups called guilds to control their industry and maintain standards.

As merchants began to travel abroad, contact with the outside world increased. And so began the next historical period, the Renaissance.

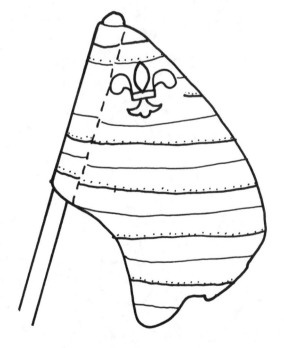

Coat of Arms

Historical Aid

Heraldic symbols were important during medieval times and were found in many aspects of life. The suit of armor made it difficult to distinguish friend from foe on the battlefield so it was a natural choice for knights to choose symbols as their marks of identification. Each knight had his own heraldic design marked on his shield, his tunic and even on the cloth covering his horse. This design was known as a *coat of arms*.

Most persons did not know how to write so in order to prove the authenticity of documents it was common to use a seal with a person's heraldic design as a signature or a way to identify a particular family. The design commemorated an event, occupation or outstanding quality in one's life. A *herald* was selected to supervise the selection of colors and symbols so there would be no duplicates.

Project

Design a family coat of arms to paint on a shield or to identify classroom "documents". Select a *herald* to review the design for duplicates and approve the final design.

Materials

- Shield pattern, reproduced for each student
- Large sheet contrasting color construction paper
- Drawing paper
- Crayons
- Tempera paint, brushes
- Scissors
- Glue

Directions

1. Create a heraldic design for a personal coat of arms. Begin by sketching and coloring a first draft of the design. Be sure the design symbolizes an interest or event in the student's life. Submit the design to the classroom *herald* for review.

2. After the design has been reviewed and approved, paint it in the shield pattern.

3. Cut out the shield when the paint has dried.

4. Glue the completed shield to contrasting construction paper.

Seals and Signets

Historical Aid

People of all classes, noblemen included, often could not read or write. Instead of signing a document they added a wax seal pressed from a metal die. The seal was sometimes incorporated into a smaller design called a *signet* and engraved into a ring. The signet ring was practical as well as decorative. The wearer simply turned his hand over and pressed his signet ring into the waiting hot wax.

The engraving in the seal often reflected a family's heraldic symbols. Occasionally they included limited letters. Military leaders also attached their seals to military orders. Seals were also used in dies for badges and medallions.

Project

Carve a die from Styrofoam to make an individualized signet ring for printing on medallions and classroom documents.

Materials

- Styrofoam meat trays
- Toothpicks
- Modeling clay
- Pipe cleaners

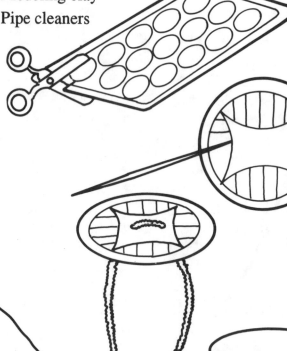

Directions

1. Cut the Styrofoam tray into one-inch circles.

2. Use toothpicks to engrave a design into the Styrofoam.

3. Poke two holes through the Styrofoam and thread a pipe cleaner through the holes.

4. Twist the pipe cleaner to fit the index finger.

5. Practice pressing the signet into modeling clay.

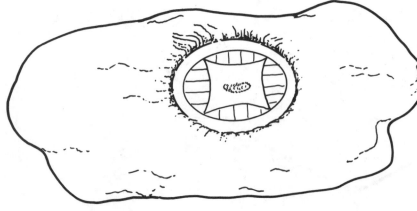

Gems and Jewels

Historical Aid

Women of medieval western Europe liked to display their rank by wearing rings and brooches. These pieces of jewelry were usually fashioned from gold with precious stones set among engraved designs of human figures and coiled monsters. Some took the shape of animals that were symbols of family lines. Wearing the brooch showed allegiance to the family.

During the latter part of the Middle Ages, jewels were also used to adorn hats and belts. Jewels encrusted the crowns of royalty and headwear of noble women.

Project

Design and make a jeweled brooch.

Directions

1. Cut a cardboard shape for the brooch. The shape should be wider or longer than the pin backing. Review the illustrations for ideas.

2. Paint the cardboard backing. While gold is preferred, any color selection is fine.

3. When the paint has dried, glue "jewels" to the cardboard shape. If costume jewelry is not available to take apart, roll tissue paper wads in bead shapes or use puffy paints to create dimension.

4. Glue the pin backing to the cardboard.

Materials

- Pin backs (available in bead or hobby shops)
- Recycled costume jewelry, beads, sequins
- Hot glue or tacky glue
- Cardboard or poster board
- Gold or other paint, brushes
- Puffy paint (optional)
- Tissue paper in a variety of colors

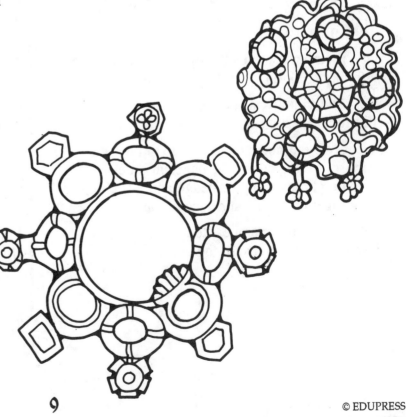

Manuscripts

Historical Aid

During the Middle Ages, manuscripts were written on parchment and, later, on paper called *vellum*. Monks worked in a special place in the monasteries called the *scriptorium* and produced most of the books.

Manuscript production was highly specialized. One group of monks prepared the vellum and a second group did the writing. A third group decorated the manuscripts (see Illuminations, page 11). Finally, a fourth group of monks put the finished manuscripts in the library, sold them or traded them to other monasteries.

Most books produced during the Middle Ages were Bibles or other religious books. Nonreligious books included books about beasts called *bestiaries*, romances and the works of ancient Greek and Roman authors.

Project

Form cooperative groups of four to six members to produce a manuscript complete with illuminations and binding.

Materials

- White typing paper or other lightweight paper
- Crayons, watercolors or marking pens
- Black ink pens
- Hole puncher
- Shoelace or yarn

Directions

1. Work together to write a *bestiary*—a tale about an imaginary or legendary medieval beast. Divide the tale into equal parts, one for each group member.

2. Each member rewrites their part of the story with black ink on white typing paper.

3. Work individually or in pairs to decorate (illuminate) each page.

4. Select two members of the group to bind the manuscript by placing the pages in order, punching holes along one edge and "stitching" them together with a shoelace or yarn.

5. Select two more members to read the manuscript to the rest of the class.

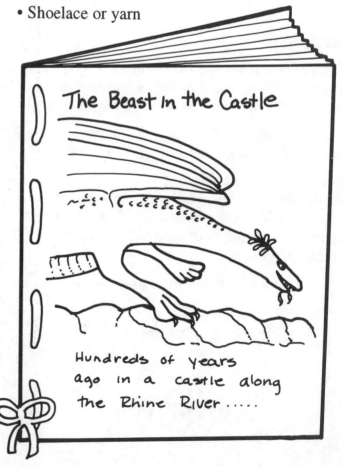

The Beast In the Castle

Hundreds of years ago in a castle along the Rhine River.....

Illuminations

Many manuscripts of the Middle Ages were beautifully decorated with pictures or designs in a variety of colors. Often, gold or silver leaf was used on the initial letters and the decoration. These pictures, designs and decorations on a manuscript page were called *illuminations*. The bright and gilded colors of the manuscripts, indeed, appeared illuminated. Different styles of illumination developed throughout Europe. All, however, used six basic forms: animals, branches with leaves or berries, geometric designs, ornamental letters, braids and scrollwork.

Some illuminators were monks, others were professional painters, both women and men. Their miniature pictures added interest and were helpful in telling the story.

Project

Create an illumination in the form of an ornamental alphabet letter.

Materials

• Half-sheet white construction paper

• Paint, markers and/or crayons

• Gold and silver ink pens

Directions

1. Sketch the outline of the first initial of your last name in a large block letter on the construction paper. Outline the letter in dark crayon.

2. Paint or color a design inside the outline.

3. Use gold or silver ink pens or a combination of the two to add detail inside the letter.

4. Decorate with crayons and pens around the letter, too.

Castles

Historical Aid

A castle was the home and fortress of a feudal lord. They were built to protect those who lived in or near them from thieves, rival lords and invaders from other lands. Servants, soldiers, priests, tailors and bakers worked within the castle walls. The first castles were built from wood, but were later replaced by stone construction and surrounded by thick stone walls. Those with two walls, one inside the other, were called *concentric*. There were round or square towers where the walls met. The main tower, with walls as thick as nine feet (three meters), was called the *keep* where the castle's lord, his family and his knights ate and slept. There were several wooden floors each with a large fireplace and connected by a spiral staircase.

Toward the end of the Middle Ages, castles became very grand with more elaborate furnishings, window designs and interior design.

Project

Form cooperative groups to construct a model of a castle.

Materials

- Resource and picture books about castles
- Castle building suggestions, following page
- Cardboard
- Milk cartons
- Yarn or string
- Marking pens
- Construction paper
- Scissors
- Glue
- Toothpicks
- Student-supplied materials of choice

Directions

1. Form cooperative groups. Give each group a copy of the building suggestions on the following page. Each should have a large cardboard base.

2. Brainstorm ways to add detail to the castles. Encourage students to be creative in their use of materials and ideas while making the castle as authentic as possible.
   - Use markers to draw stone walls or collect and glue small stones to the outside of walls and towers.
   - Build toothpick ladders.
   - Make toothpick and paper banners to fly from castle towers.

Castle Keep and Towers

The lord and his family lived in the keep on several floors. There were other towers at each corner of the castle. There were holes in the thick tower walls to shoot arrows through.

Make a tower by cutting one side out of a milk carton. Cover with construction paper. Cut arrow openings in the sides. Cut cardboard floors to add inside.

Castle Walls

The walls around the castle were very thick. Soldiers could stand upon them.

Cut castle walls from cardboard. Notch the tops. Draw or glue stones.

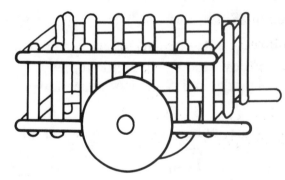

Inner Ward

The space in the center of the castle was called the inner ward. It was here the business of the castle was carried out.

Create a scene that reflects castle life. Make miniature knights polishing their armor. Stack small boxes to resemble hay bales. Make a small cart with wagon wheels pulling a cargo of vegetables.

Gatehouse and Drawbridge

When a doorway was built in a wall it had U-shaped towers on each side. The opening was covered by an iron gate and led to a bridge that could be pulled up during an attack.

Cut an arch in the castle wall. Make two round towers and place one on each side. Criss-cross black construction paper to make a gate.

Cut a rectangular cardboard drawbridge and hang it at the gate with yarn.

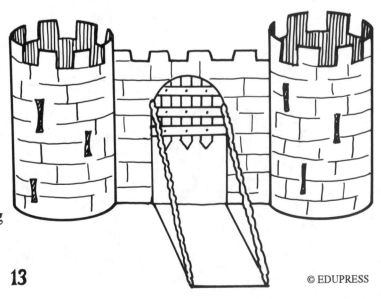

Attack and Defend

Historical Aid

Within the castle walls lived knights and soldiers who were ready to defend their home. Every castle was stocked with provisions to last for six months. A siege could last that long and starving castle inhabitants was a common tactic. Attackers used a variety of giant catapults that hurled rocks over castle walls. Movable towers enabled attackers to get to the top of castle walls. Battering rams were used to smash down the castle gate. Attackers set scaling ladders against or tunneled beneath the castle walls. Inside the castle, the fighting was hand to hand with shields, crossbows, swords, mace clubs and axes.

Castle defenders poured rocks and boiling oil or water on the attackers. Arrows were aimed through specially cut openings in castle walls. It wasn't until the 1400s that cannons became a popular form of defense and attack.

Project

Make and test a model of a medieval attack or defense method. Explain the purpose and evaluate its effectiveness.

Directions

1. Reproduce and cut apart several sets of project cards. Allow students to decide if they will build a model individually or cooperatively in pairs or triads.

2. Review the contents of each project card. Have groups (or individuals) decide which model they want to construct.

3. Students may select materials from the supply table (stocked with items from the material list) or provide their own in order to construct a model of a medieval attack or defense weapon.

4. Allow time for students to test and evaluate their models.

Materials

- Project cards, following
- Tall milk cartons
- Craft sticks
- Paper tubes
- Cardboard
- Scissors
- Glue
- String or twine
- Construction paper
- Student-supplied materials

Embrasure

An **embrasure** was an alcove in the castle wall, with a narrow opening to the outside which allowed defenders to shoot arrows without exposing themselves to enemies.

Cut an opening, as shown, in the cardboard. How far and accurately can you toss a wad of paper through the opening?

Battering Ram

A **battering ram** was a heavy beam of wood with a ram's head at the end. Men ran to the wall, beating again and again at the same spot, trying to make an opening in it.

Wrap the end of a wooden dowel or cardboard tube with a sock stuffed with newspaper. What can you knock over?

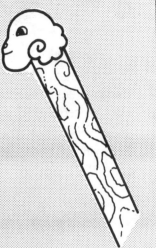

Siege Tower

The best way to get to the top of the castle wall was with a **siege tower**, a wooden shed, several stories high, set on rollers. It was covered with animal skins to prevent burning.

Use milk cartons and craft sticks to construct a siege tower. Can you propel toy soldiers over the top of a pile of books?

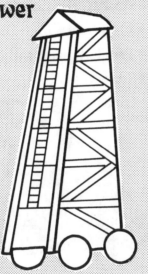

Trebuchet

A **trebuchet** had an arm up to 60 feet (80 meters) long and could sling giant stones up to 980 feet (300 meters).

Use craft sticks and string to build a trebuchet with a sling pouch at the end of a long arm. Test the slinging capabilities with objects of varying weight. (Be safety conscious!)

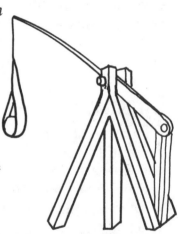

Catapult

The **catapult** had a wooden arm with a cup at one end that, when released, could fling rocks, flaming rags, dead animals and other disease spreaders.

Use cardboard, craft sticks and twine to make a catapult. Test the distance you can propel objects such as marshmallows and small rocks. (Be safety conscious!)

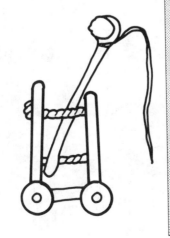

Siege Bow

Siege bows, or **ballistas,** were large mounted crossbows that shot huge arrows when the large bow arm was pulled back.

Cut a cardboard bow. Add a tight rope to each end. Cut a large cardboard arrow and test its shooting ability.

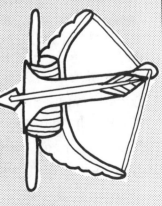

Portcullis

The first defense an enemy might encounter when attacking a castle was a moat and drawbridge. The second was a *portcullis*. The portcullis was a heavy wooden and iron grating that protected the entrance to a castle. It was made from criss-crossed bars of wood. The wooden bars were clad in iron to strengthen them. Spikes were formed at the bottom.

On the first floor of the castle tower, there was a room in which a gatekeeper stood guard. From here, the portcullis, connected by chains to a winch, could be lowered into position at a moment's notice.

Project

Construct a portcullis to use on a painting depicting life inside the castle walls.

Materials

- Black and white construction paper
- Tempera paint and brushes
- Scissors
- Glue

Directions

1. Paint a castle courtyard scene on white construction paper. You might show peasants at work or knights shining their armor. While the paint dries, make a portucullis.

2. Cut the length of the black construction paper into ½ inch wide (1.27 cm) strips.

3. Overlap the strips to create a grid. Space the strips evenly apart, allowing at least ½ inch (1.27 cm) between them. Glue the grid together where the strips intersect.

4. Cut the bottom of each bar into a pointed shape to resemble a spike.

5. Glue the portcullis over the dry, painted scene. Cut the top into an arch.

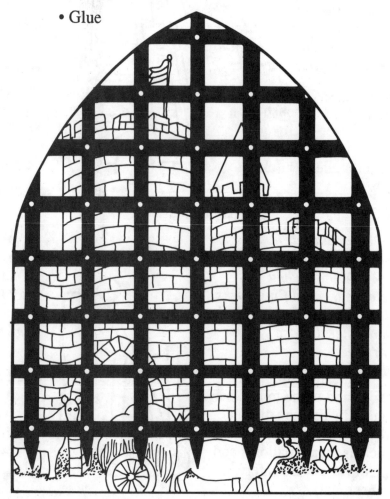

Great Hall

The great hall was the main room in a castle. It was used for eating, sleeping and conducting business. It was often connected to the kitchen by a long passageway. In the evening, there were suppers and entertainment. It wasn't until the thirteenth century that the lord built extra rooms for himself and his family, away from the rest of the household.

It was in the great hall that a feast took place. Tables and benches—not chairs—were set up along the sides of the hall. A fire blazed in the center and tapestries covered the stone walls. If royalty was present, a high table was placed at the end of the hall and stood on a raised platform. The lord displayed his finest gold goblets and plates.

Project

Transform your classroom into a great hall for your medieval feast (see pages 18-20).

Materials

- Brown butcher paper
- White butcher paper
- Napkins
- Paper cups
- Several small bowls
- Salt
- Plastic spoons

Directions

1. Move all the desks or tables end-to-end along two walls at opposite sides of the room. Arrange chairs on both sides. (You will have to *pretend* you are sitting on benches!)

2. Place one table at the end of the two rows of desks, to form a U-shape.

3. Roll five to seven brown butcher paper logs. Stack them to "build a fire" in the center of the room.

4. Cover the tables with white butcher paper. Put a napkin, spoon and cup at each seat.

5. Pour salt into bowls and place them at intervals on the tables.

Medieval Feast

The lord and lady of a manor hosted great feasts in the castle hall. The food was plentiful and elegantly presented. Beef and mutton (sheep) were stewed with onions, garlic and herbs. Venison (deer), swans, geese and quail were roasted. Pastry, called a *coffin*, was filled with a mixture of meat, dates, ginger, vinegar, eggs and herbs.

At royal meals, a peacock was cooked and reassembled with its feathers in place. Apples, pears, figs, grapes, oranges and lemons were picked from the castle gardens. Cheese was made and butter was churned. Fish was served Wednesday, Friday and Saturday. Common vegetables were dried peas and beans. Chefs created spectacular desserts of sugar paste, marzipan and jelly painted and molded into shapes like castles or ships. Milk was used chiefly for cooking such things as fine almond puddings.

Project

Use the ideas and recipes on this and the following three pages to plan and prepare a medieval feast. Choose a lord and lady to oversee the efforts. The rest of the class will be the serfs in charge of the preparations.

Materials

• See individual recipes and preparation ideas

Directions

1. Divide into four cooperative groups. Assign three of the groups to be in charge of fixing something from the menu for the class.

2. Assign the fourth group the job of preparing the great hall for the feast (see page 17).

3. Choose people to carry out the jobs on the job list found on page 19. Change jobs part of the way through the feast so that everyone has a chance to dine.

4. Select a king to be seated at the royal table.

Medieval Feast

There were many jobs that needed to be done during a feast. Look at the descriptions below and assign the jobs to class members. They will be in charge of assembling the materials and carrying out the job. The materials needed, if any, are printed in **bold letters.**

Serfs

The serfs lived in huts provided for them on the lord's estate. In return, they were bound to serve the lord. When the time came for a royal feast, the serfs handled all the preparations and serving during the meal. They carried food from the kitchen, served trenchers (see page 21) and scooped stew with a ladle. They offered fruit trays to the guests, cleared the trenchers and served dessert.

Ewerer

There were no forks, but napkins were provided. Some food was eaten with spoons, but many people ate with their fingers. They used their little fingers to sprinkle salt from the bowls *(saltcellars)* to their food.

The Ewerer brought a **pitcher of water**, a **large bowl** and **towel** between courses so diners could wash their hands.

The Ewerer also tasted the water before pouring it over the king's hands.

Jugglers

The feast was not complete without entertainment for the diners while they ate. Minstrels played **musical instruments** and sang, jesters told amusing stories and jugglers showed their skills with **juggling balls.**

Panter

The Panter had a very special assignment. He was the king's personal servant. He was in charge of seeing to the king's dining needs. The Panter carried special **trays** to bring food, trenchers and saltcellar to the king.

Trumpeter and Drummer

The feast did not begin until the trumpeter announced the arrival of the king with fanfare from his **trumpet.** After the king was seated, the trumpeter again sounded his trumpet to indicate the start of the feast.

The trumpeter blew his horn and the drummer beat on his **drum** between each food course.

Fruit Platter

Needs:
- Plastic knives
- Trays

Preparation:
Wash, dry and slice oranges, apples and pears. Arrange them on a tray around a cluster of grapes.

Beef Stew

Needs:
- Crock pot
- Two pounds stewing beef, cut in cubes
- Two eight-ounce jars beef gravy
- Salt, pepper, crushed thyme, herbs of choice
- Onions (optional)
- Large spoon and ladle

Preparation:
Mix the beef and gravy in a crock pot. Add seasonings and herbs to taste. Cut onions into thin wedges and add to stew mixture in crock pot. (The addition of onions makes the recipe more authentic, but is optional depending on student tastes!) Cook on high for four hours or until meat is tender.

12 small servings

Almond Pudding

Needs:
- Large mixing bowl
- Two large packages *instant* vanilla pudding
- Milk (check package for amount)
- Almond extract
- Hand or electric egg beater
- Measuring cups and spoons

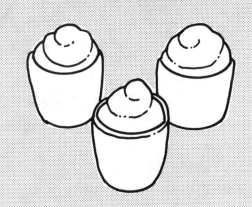

Preparation:
Prepare pudding according to package directions. Add a small spoonful almond extract.

16 small servings

Bread Plates

Historical Aid

The finest grains were grown at local manors, ground into flour at the lord's mill and baked into bread in the castle kitchen or bakehouse. Some grains were used to bake *trenchers,* flat, coarse bread made from whole wheat.

Stale trenchers were used as dining plates. The trenchers soaked up the gravy from stews. The peasants ate their gravy-soaked trenchers while the wealthy gave theirs to the poor or fed them to the dogs.

Project

Work in small groups to mix, roll and bake trenchers to use as plates during a classroom medieval feast.

Directions

1. The recipe will make eight (8) trenchers. Work in groups this size to mix and make the trenchers. Each group will need the ingredients and materials listed.

2. Tear off a piece of aluminum foil for each student, large enough to roll the dough into a medium-sized plate.

3. Follow the recipe directions in the box.

Materials

- 2 cups (473 ml) sifted all-purpose flour
- 3 teaspoons (14.7 ml) baking powder
- Rolling pins and/or aluminum pie tins
- ¼ cup (59 ml) shortening
- ½ teaspoon (2.45 ml) salt

- ¾ cup (177 ml) milk   • Large bowl
- Fork   • Measuring cups
- Aluminum foil   • Oven

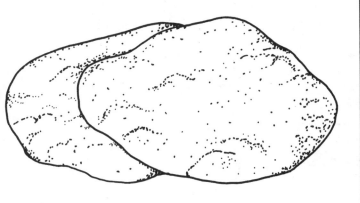

• Directions

- *Use a fork to cut the shortening into the flour to make course crumbs.*

- *Make a well in the dough and pour in the milk. Stir with a fork.*

- *Divide the dough into eight equal pieces.*

- *Knead the dough on the aluminum foil 12 times with the palm of the hand. Roll with a rolling pin or flatten with the bottom of a pie tin to about ½ inch (1.25 cm) thick.*

- *Bake on the aluminum foil at 450 degrees for 12 minutes.*

Pottery

Historical Aid

Typical medieval pottery was finished with a green glaze. Crude pottery jugs were used to carry ale or wine for the ordinary diners in the great hall. In order to make the jugs more attractive, potters often molded faces or animals into the surface. A jug's legs might have resembled animal feet. The spout was sometimes shaped like an animal's head through which the jug's contents was poured into equally crude mugs. Often two diners would share a bowl or cup.

Eventually jugs were made from copper alloy. It was still characteristic, however, for them to feature animal characteristics as part of its design.

Project

Make a pottery jug or mug.

Materials

- Self-hardening clay
- Green paint, brushes
- Clear lacquer spray
- Toothpicks, for engraving

Directions

1. Students may choose to shape a mug or jug from the clay. Use toothpicks and clay to engrave and shape animal features on the sculpted piece.

2. Paint the mug or jug green after the clay has hardened. Spray with clear lacquer.

Troubadour

Historical Aid

People of the Middle Ages were great lovers of poetry and legends. As they could not read, a storyteller or recitalist of verses was very popular. Wandering musicians, poets and storytellers, known as *troubadours,* traveled through the land entertaining lords and ladies with tales of love, chivalrous deeds and the bravery of knights.

Many castles had a troubadour of its own who resided there and entertained guests after dinner. The troubadour accompanied himself on the lute or some other musical instrument. Recitals of romantic tales and lengthy poems centered around the name of a favorite hero were especially popular. King Arthur and his Knights of the Round Table, Robin Hood of Sherwood Forest and Saint George and the Dragon were particularly favorite subjects.

Project

Videotape an oral presentation based on a troubadour's talents—tell a story, recite a poem or sing a song about medieval people and life.

Materials

- Video camera
- Literature selections featuring legends about dragons and knights (see Literature List, page 3)
- Musical instruments such as an autoharp, drums, recorder or stringed instruments

Directions

1. Form cooperative pairs of students. Together, the student pairs find or write a legend, poem or song about medieval times.

2. Have the pairs of students practice their presentations. One presents the material, the other accompanies on a musical instrument.

3. Videotape the presentations.

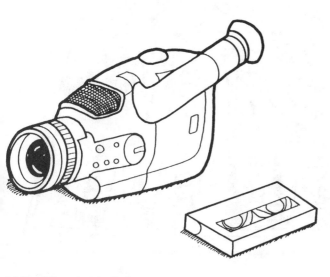

Games

People of all classes gathered in the great hall of the castle for meals and entertainment. Board games such as checkers and backgammon were popular among all the people. Children played a board game called Foxes and Geese. Chess was a favorite because it had a mock battlefield where players could develop strategy and pieces could attack each other. Marbles and horseshoes were other popular activities. Adult's even played children's games such as Blindman's Bluff.

Boys' games taught them how to behave like knights. One game was called Robber and another The King Doesn't Lie. Boys also made hobbyhorses and showed off for girls by charging at each other.

Project

Learn to play one or more of the popular medieval board games.

Materials

- Checkers and checkerboard
- Backgammon board
- Marbles
- Chess board
- Horseshoes
- Carpet squares

Directions

1. Set up an area in the classroom where board games can be played. If there is room, set several carpet squares on the floor and establish an area for marbles.

2. Team one student who knows how to play a game with one who doesn't. Discuss and implement peer-group teaching with the students.

3. Establish an area outside where horseshoes can be learned and played. Discuss safety rules.

4. Invite children to create their own rules for games such as Robber and The King Doesn't Lie. Have them think about how a medieval child might have played the same game.

Clothing

Historical Aid

Men and women of the early Middle Ages wore simple tunics, called *surcoats,* made from linen or wool. A knight wore a sleeved undertunic of linen or wool, reaching below the knees. Over this was a sleeveless tunic, open at the sides and fastened with a belt. Men wore loose breeches or long stockings of bright colors under their tunics. The woman's tunic developed into a long dress with oversized armholes and worn over a long-sleeved gown. Cloaks were often worn over the tunics.

Clothes for the wealthy became more colorful in the 1300s. Dozens of buttons decorated the outer garments. The surcoat was edged with fur. The sleeves buttoned tightly from wrist to elbow. Jeweled felt hats and capes lined in fur were popular. Shoes became so pointed that the front was curled up and fastened to the knee with a small jeweled chain.

Project

Make a decorated surcoat for boys *and* girls.

Directions

1. Cut two armholes and a neck hole from the sides and stitched end of a pillowcase.

2. Draw or paint a design or crest on the front. Stitch or glue buttons and/or fur trim.

3. Wear the surcoat over a turtleneck or t-shirt. Wear a leather belt around the waist.

Materials

- Pillowcase
- Scissors
- Turtleneck shirt or t-shirt
- Fabric markers or paints
- Buttons
- Fake fur (optional)
- Needle and thread

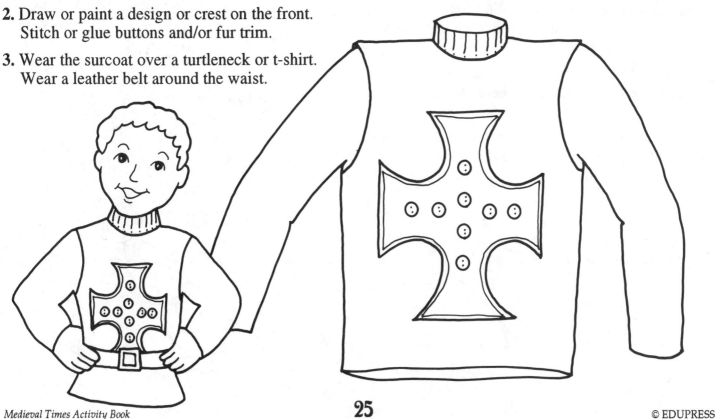

Headwear

Historical Aid

Throughout medieval times, hats were often worn to indicate social status. Head coverings worn by the lower classes, as they toiled in the fields, provided much needed protection from harsh weather. Kings and church officials wore headwear to indicate their position of authority. And, of course, knights wore armor to protect their heads in combat.

During the 1100s and 1200s women wore metal hair nets, veils and draped throat covers called *wimples* which were worn with various hood-like coverings. Men wore hoods that had long tails called *liripipes*. By the 1300s people began to wear hats for decoration resulting in a large variety of hat styles. Eastern influences resulted in hats that resembled turbans. During the 1400s many European women wore a tall cone-shaped hat with a streaming veil.

Project

Design a medieval head covering based on historical information.

Directions

1. Reproduce and give each child a copy of the Medieval Headwear information page. Review its contents. They may look through books for other ideas, too.

2. Create a hat or form of headwear based on the pictures and information gathered from materials of choice.

3. As an extended activity, students may assume the identity of a person who might have worn the hat and share an aspect of their medieval life.

Materials

• Medieval Headwear information page, following
• Assorted fabrics
• Trims such as fur, sequins and lace
• Pliable wire
• White glue and tacky glue
• Stapler
• Construction paper
• Scissors
• Illustrated books about medieval times

Troubadour

This hat of cloth with a rolled band and sometimes a long tail was worn by troubadours, jesters and other entertainers.

Villein

The hard-working villeins (peasants and castle servants) protected their heads with draped fabric or caps.

Ladies in Waiting

Attendants to the lady of the manor wore a cloth draped over their head and held in place with a rolled fabric band. Embroidery and jewels were sometimes added.

Lord and Lady

Decorative fabric hats were rolled and stacked resembling turbans. Fur, jewels and lace-like trims were added for further decoration.

Noble Woman

Jewel-encrusted metal hair nets were fashioned to fit over the top and sides of the head.

Page

A boy of noble birth, training to become a knight, wore a hat similar to an upside down bowl.

Women of the Realm

A cone shaped hat called a *hennin* was worn during the 1400s. It measured from 3 to 4 feet (0.9 to 1.2 meters) high and had a long, floating veil.

King and Queen

A royal crown was worn as a symbol of supreme authority. This circular headwear was usually made of gold, engraved and ornamented with precious gems.

Knights and Knighthood

Historical Aid

A young boy training to be a knight spent the first years of his life with his family learning to ride a pony and care for horses. When seven, he became a *page* in a nobleman's household where he learned to hunt, play chess and practice chivalrous behavior. He also served meals to castle diners. At 14, he was given a sword and became a *squire*. He trained for battle and the joust and performed important castle tasks such as pouring the wine or carving the meat. He acted as a personal servant to a knight. He cleaned and assisted the knight by donning his armor. At 21, when training was complete he was knighted in a ceremony called the *accolade*. Dressed in a white shirt, gold tunic and purple cloak, a squire knelt before the man knighting him who tapped him with a sword on each shoulder and stated, "Be thou a knight." After the 1100s this distinction also brought with it independence and a parcel of land.

Project

Make a four-part accordion-fold picture showing the progressive steps to becoming a knight. Conduct a knighting ceremony and award **Knight Of The Realm** certificates.

Materials

- Two large sheets white construction paper
- Crayons
- Clear tape

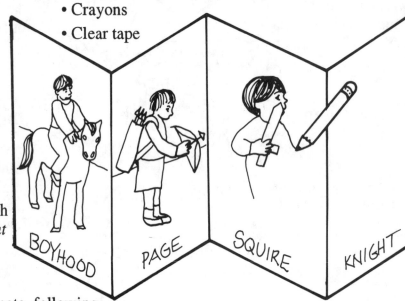

Directions

1. Fold each piece of construction paper in half, widthwise.

2. Tape them together end-to-end making an accordion-fold at the tape connection.

3. Illustrate a step toward knighthood on each page—*early boyhood, page, squire, knight*

Knighting Ceremony

- Reproduce copies of the knighthood certificate, following.
- Cut a cardboard sword in shape shown below.
- Purple fabric cape (optional)

Have students wear white, place a purple cape around their shoulders, and touch them on each shoulder with the sword. State the words of knighthood (see Historical Aid above). Present each knight, boys and girls alike, with a certificate.

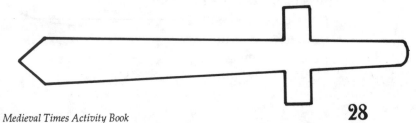

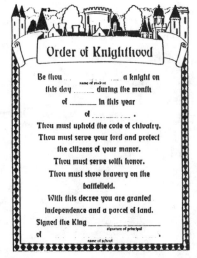

Order of Knighthood

Be thou _____ name of student _____ a knight on
this day _____ during the month
of _____ in this year
of _____.
Thou must uphold the code of chivalry.
Thou must serve your lord and protect
the citizens of your manor.
Thou must serve with honor.
Thou must show bravery on the
battlefield.
With this decree you are granted
independence and a parcel of land.
Signed the King _____
signature of principal
of _____
name of school

Order of Knighthood

Be thou _____ a knight on
name of student
this day _____ during the month

of _____ in this year

of _____ .

Thou must uphold the code of chivalry.

Thou must serve your lord and protect

the citizens of your manor.

Thou must serve with honor.

Thou must show bravery on the

battlefield.

With this decree you are granted

independence and a parcel of land.

Signed the King _____
signature of principal
of _____ .
name of school

Armor

A knight wore a full metal bodysuit called *armor* for protection in combat or displays of skill. Because the outcome of a battle depended not only on the skill of the knight, but also on the strength of his armor. Armorers (makers of armor) became respected craft workers.

A knight was dressed in armor by his squire, who always worked from the feet up. The last thing to go on was the helmet. While a helmet usually weighed between 3 to 7 pounds (1 ½ to 3 kg) some weighed over 16 pounds (7.4 kg). It was strapped to the body armor so the knight's shoulders bore the incredible weight. The helmet had a visor that opened like a door. In the 1500s it was fashionable to decorate the visors on helmets worn at tournaments. A knight's helmet had a crest of feathers or other light material.

Project

Make a knight's helmet to wear at a tournament.

Materials

- Black construction paper or tagboard
- Pencil
- Large sheet construction paper, color of choice
- Two metal brads
- Stapler
- Glue
- Pattern, following three pages

Directions

1. Cut out the pattern pieces.

2. Place the pattern fold along the fold of paper and trace. Cut out along the outline without cutting the fold.

3. Assemble the helmet as shown in the illustrations at right. Use the rectangle-shaped pattern on page 33 for size extension.

4. Use metal brads to attach the visor to the helmet at points A and B.

5. Cut a large feather from the colored paper. Staple it to the helmet.

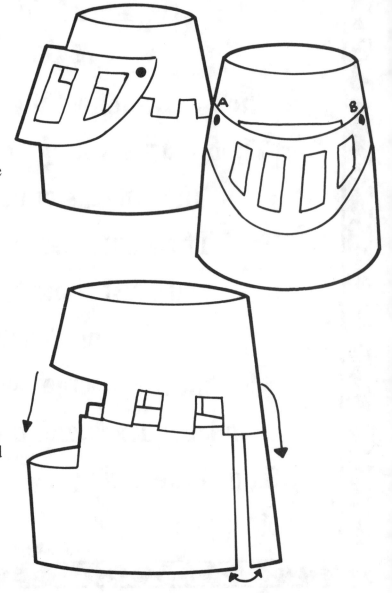

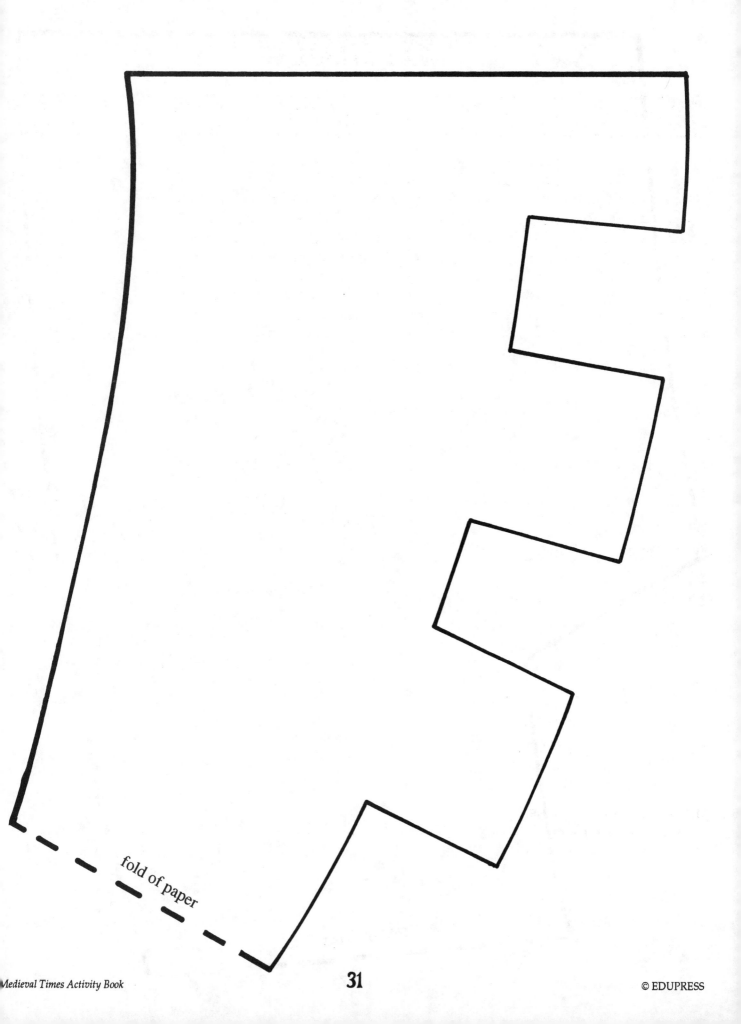

fold of paper

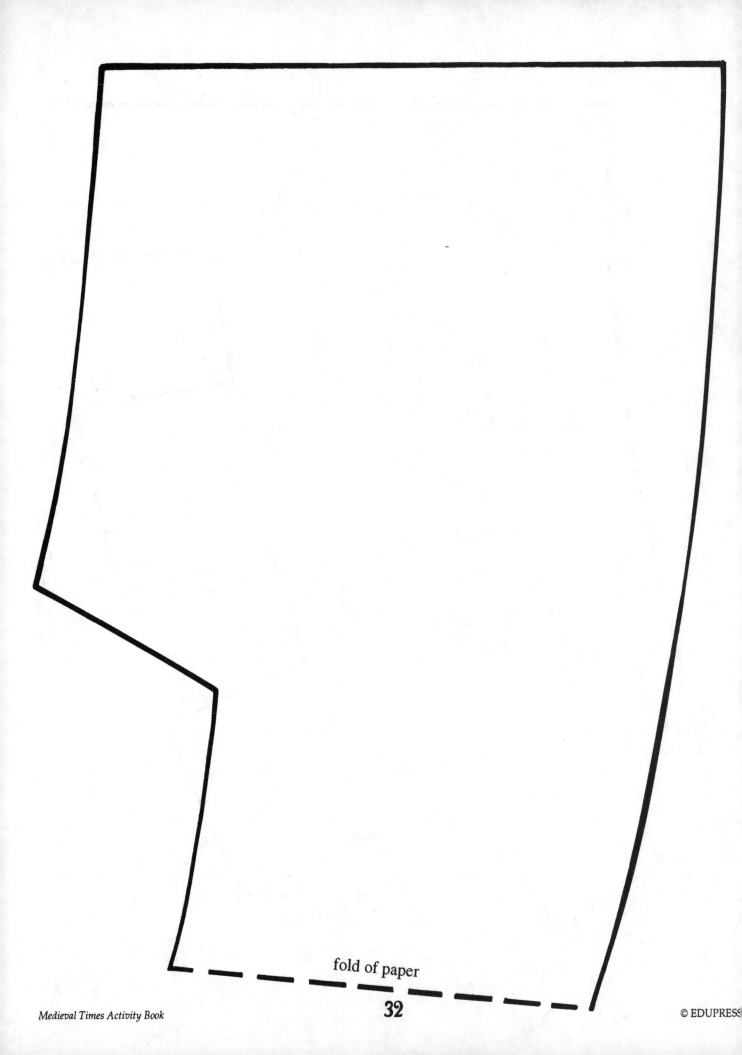

fold of paper

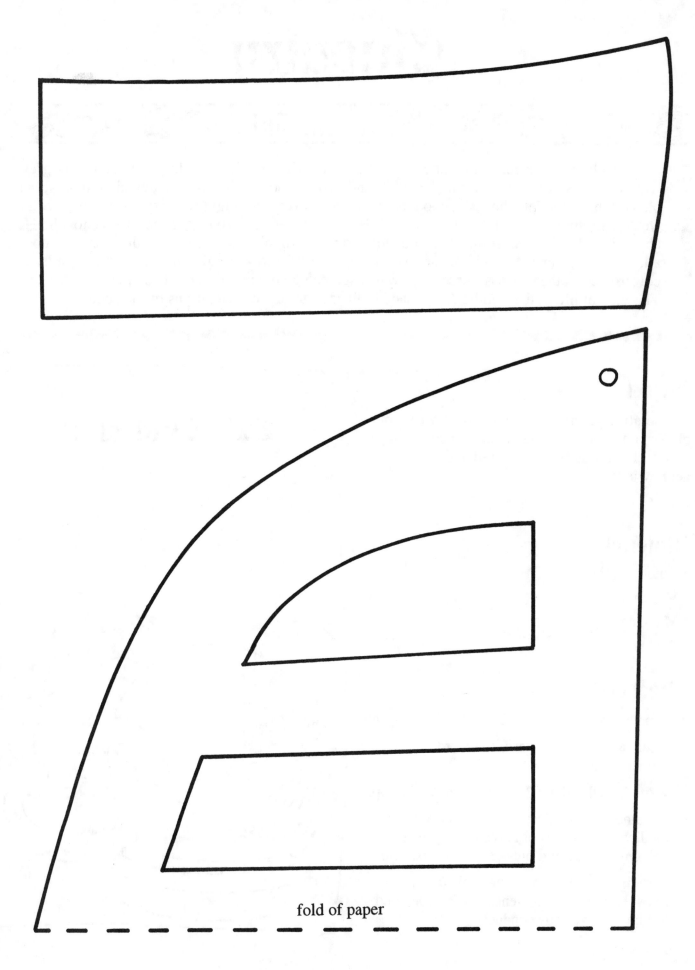

fold of paper

Chivalry

Historical Aid

Chivalry was the code, rules and values that guided a knight's life. The code of chivalry grew with the songs of the minstrels in the 1000s and 1100s. The code included a devotion to duty, fair play on the battlefield, honesty, good manners and bravery. A knight was expected to protect the weak and show respect toward women. He was to be generous and courteous to all. He championed right against injustice and evil and never flinched in the face of the enemy. Above all, a knight defended the church and was ready to die for it. A knight who was proved guilty of cowardice or other serious misconduct was disgraced by having his sword and his spurs broken. The violent life of the Middle Ages made it difficult to prevent violations of the code.

Project

Cooperatively, write a code of chivalry for your classroom. Conduct "round table" discussions in which chivalrous acts are shared and acknowledged.

Materials

- Butcher paper
- Marking pens
- Masking tape

Directions

1. Tape a large sheet of butcher paper to the wall.

2. Select a scribe (secretary) to record all information.

3. Write CODE OF CHIVALRY across the top.

4. Together, create a list of rules, based on medieval standards of chivalry, to govern behavior inside and outside your classroom.

5. Participate in weekly round table discussions to evaluate the effectiveness of the code and to honor chivalrous conduct.

Code of Chivalry

Jousting

In the 1200s, knights met in assemblies called round tables. Jousting, a contest between two knights on horseback, was a popular activity at these meetings. The knights charged at each other on horseback with heavy, blunt lances and shields and tried to knock each other to the ground. Both wore armor and their horses were covered in embroidered cloth. The wooden lances splintered easily on impact. Many mock battles were held.

A joust could also be a form of "trial by combat" in which a man accused of a crime might prove his innocence in victory. Several jousts comprised a tournament and the victorious knight was often granted great honors and prizes.

Project

Make a safe, lightweight jousting lance for use in tournament games (see pages 36-37).

Materials

- Paper tubing from gift-wrapping or paper towels
- Wide tape
- Crepe paper (optional)
- Construction paper
- Tempera paint and brushes

Directions

1. If you have paper tubing from rolls of gift-wrapping, the length is satisfactory. If you are using paper towel tubing, tape several together end-to-end to achieve the desired length.

2. Paint the paper tubing to match the chosen colors of the tournament teams (see page 36). Wrap the tubing with crepe paper to make candy cane stripes (optional).

3. Make a cone from a half-sheet of construction paper. The smaller opening should be able to slide over the paper tube. Secure the cone in place about eight inches (20.32 cm) from one end.

4. Pinch the tube closed at the opposite end.

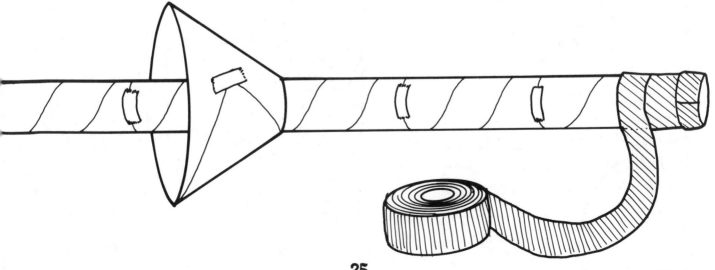

Tournament

Knights practiced their skill during peacetime by competing against each other in mock battles called *tournaments*. The main event was the joust. Archery competitions, wrestling matches and sword fights were also staged. Scores were kept by the heralds who assisted a marshal with judging. Both knight and horse wore their crests and colors. Colorful shields and banners representing the knights flew from the grandstands. There was a special gallery for the ladies with a seat of honor for the "Queen of Love and Beauty". Sometimes they wore a "favor", a scarf or handkerchief belonging to a lady who favored the man. The winner of a particular event would present the favor to his lady, tied on his lance. In some tournaments, winners were entitled to the loser's horse, armor and weapons—items of considerable value in those times.

Project

Participate in a tournament with activities drawn from medieval life.

Events

The materials needed as well as playing and scoring rules are listed under each event suggestion on the next page.

Getting Started

1. Choose two heralds and one marshal to be judges and keep score. Choose a Queen of Love and Beauty to watch the competition from a seat of honor (a chair decorated with crepe paper streamers).

2. Divide the rest of the class into two teams. Have each team select colors and design and paint a butcher paper banner for the team and a cardboard shield for each participant.

3. Make jousting lances (see page 35).

4. The marshal, heralds and Queen of Love and Beauty may select the games and events to be staged and determine their scoring rules and order of competition.

Banner

Shield

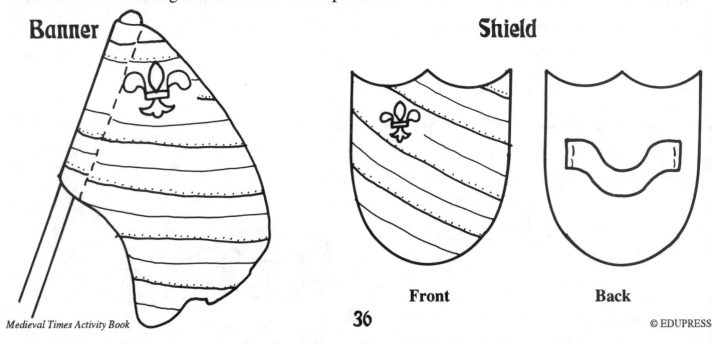

Front　　　　**Back**

Ball Toss

A common medieval game was playing catch with a ball made of leather or cloth stuffed with almost anything! Sometimes the ball was hit over a net or raised mound of earth with a gloved hand.

Have each team stand on opposite sides of a net. Toss a beanbag or small ball back and forth. If a team fails to make the catch, a point is scored for the opposition.

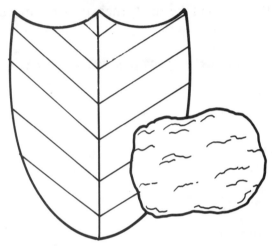

Armor Race

A squire attended the tournament to assist his knight by carrying his banner and helping him put on his many layers of armor.

Have a relay race. Gather an identical number and type of clothing for each team. Form pairs within the team. At the marshal's command, one pair from each team works to dress one of them in armor (the layers of clothing). At the marshal's approval, the clothes are removed and the next pair repeats the steps. The first team to have all its pairs finish is declared the winner.

Quintain

A quintain was similar to a crossbar with a shield on one side and a weight on the other. It was used for lance practice. The squire had to hit the shield on the crossbar and duck before the sandbag on the other end swung around and hit him.

A player from an opposing team gently tosses a beanbag at a competitor. The competitor tries to block the throw with his/her shield. Score one point for a blocked throw and one point for a throw that hits a player. The point is scored for each successful player. Allow three throws per competitive pair.

Lance Accuracy

It was important for a knight to be accurate with the thrust of his lance. In battle, it was a matter of life or death!

Hang a plastic ring from the end of a stick. Secure the stick to the crossbars of the swings or monkey bars.

Each player, in turn, charges at the ring, lance drawn! As the ring is approached, the player tries to put his/her lance through the ring, letting go of the lance as the pass is made. If the lance goes through the ring a point is scored.

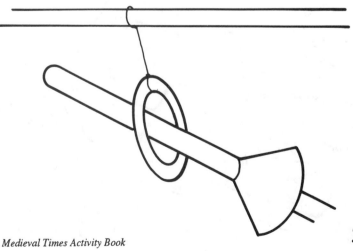

Cobblestone

Streets in a medieval town were narrow, crooked, dark and filthy. Until about 122 A.D., they were not paved. The people threw all their garbage and rubbish into the streets. Disease spread quickly and killed many.

During the 1200s, people in some towns began to pave their streets with rough cobblestones. These naturally rounded stones were carefully laid, sometimes forming a pattern, over the dirt streets. Their uneven surface made it difficult to walk on, but cobblestone streets were an improvement over the existing conditions. Townspeople began to take other measures for more sanitary conditions.

Project

Choose one of the projects and recreate a cobblestone pattern.

Materials

- Drawing paper
- Crayons

Directions

Project 1:

1. Use crayons to create a cobblestone pattern on drawing paper.
2. Try to keep the distance between the "stones" very small and even.

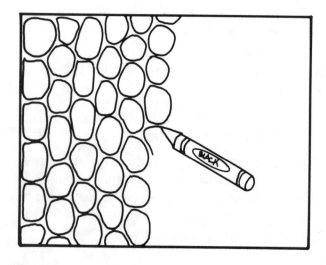

Materials

- Shoebox lid
- Rubber cement
- Stones and rocks

Directions

Project 2:

1. Gather some rocks and stones. Select the ones that are smooth and somewhat flat.
2. Try to pave the box lid with stones. How difficult is it to get an even surface and keep the stones close together?

Medieval Towns

Historical Aid

Early medieval towns were only small settlements outside the walls of a castle or a church. As the towns grew, walls were built around them which limited the amount of land available. Buildings five or six stories high stood crowded together. Since there were no sidewalks, the building fronts were lined up along the narrow, winding unpaved or cobblestone streets.

Wealthy citizens had houses of stone and brick, but most were made of wood filled with *wattle* (woven sticks) and *daub* (sealing clay or mud) with roofs of slate tiles or wooden shingles. Flags hung over businesses to identify their trade or craft. Men engaging in the same craft usually lived on the same street with the street being named accordingly—Threadneedle Street, Tanners' Row and so on. Those who ventured out at night carried torches on the dark streets.

Project

Form cooperative groups to paint a mural depicting a street scene in a medieval town.

Materials

- Butcher paper cut to size for a mural
- Pencils
- Construction paper
- Paint
- Scissors
- Glue
- Sketching pencils

Directions

1. Review pages 38 and 40 for more information on medieval streets and homes. Ask each group to make a list of what they might include in their mural.

2. Sketch a street scene on the butcher paper. Paint the final scene. Cut and glue construction paper detail to add dimension such as flags and cobblestone.

Medieval Names

Historical Aid

Often during the Middle Ages, a man came to be known by the name of his trade. A worker in metals was called a smith. If his name were John, he would come to be known around town as John, the smith. A pottery worker named David might be called David Potter. A man named James who was a fine hunter might be called James Hunter.

Many family names today have come from the trades of the Middle Ages. Such names as Carpenter, Miller, Baker, Weaver, Goldman might well be traced to medieval craftsmen.

Project

Make a personalized puppet that reflects your surname or a fictitious surname that relates to a medieval craft.

Directions

1. Discuss the last names of class members. Make a list of those related to a craft or profession. Look through phone books and make lists of other surnames related to crafts and professions.

2. Make a stick puppet that reflects the student as if he or she were a craftsman in the Middle Ages. The puppet should depict the student's last name or the one selected from the phone book.

3. Present a puppet show in which each puppet tells a little about their medieval craft.

Materials

- Telephone books
- Construction paper
- Scissors
- Glue
- Fabric scraps
- Craft (popsicle) stick

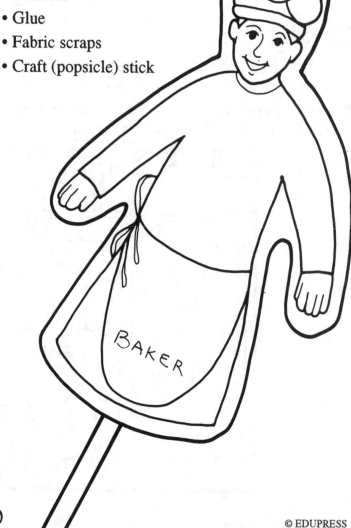

Market Place Banner

Historical Aid

Once or twice a year a town might hold a fair to which merchants came from distant places to sell their wares. During this time, tumblers and minstrels, trained bears and horses would perform their tricks. Markets were held in the town square one or two days each week.

Everyday life was quite different. The shops of craftsmen lined the streets. The shops were similar to booths with shutters that opened during market hours. Here, on the first floor of their home, the craftsmen were busy at work and offered their items for sale. Hanging over the shop doors were signs with painted pictures suggesting the business of the shop owner—a boot for the cobbler, a ring for the goldsmith, bread for the baker, and so on.

Project

Design and make a shop owner's sign.

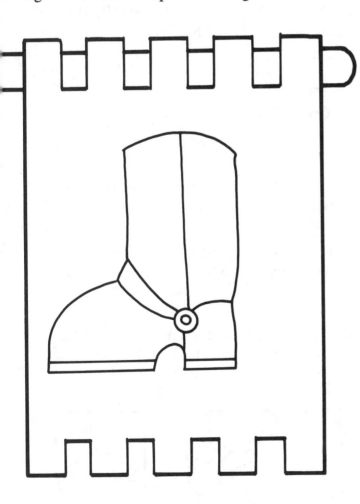

Materials

- Large sheet white construction paper
- Paint stirrer (available at paint stores)
- Paint
- Scissors
- Glue

Directions

1. Decide on a profession or craft to depict in a sign.

2. Determine an object or picture that would symbolize that craft or profession.

3. Sketch the object vertically on the construction paper, leaving a two-inch (5.08 cm) margin at the top. Cut the top margin as shown in the illustration.

4. Paint the final sketch.

5. Paint the paint stirrer a corresponding color. Glue the banner to the paint stick.

Guilds

Historical Aid

During the thirteenth, fourteenth and fifteenth centuries, town craftsmen formed associations called *guilds* according to the kind of work they did. There were guilds of carpenters, weavers, millers, butchers, bakers, grocers, tailors, goldsmiths, armorers, masons and shoemakers. No one was allowed to engage in a craft unless they were a guild member. Officers were chosen, dues were levied and honesty in trade was monitored. A guild helped its members by caring for its sick and poor.

Important guilds had their own halls in which guild business was conducted. Each guild had a banner on which the emblems showing the tools of their craft and their motto were displayed. Guild members had uniforms, called *livery*, which they wore when meeting. The livery was usually of two colors, scarlet and green, black or deep blue.

Project

Form cooperative groups to make a guild livery, a uniform representing a medieval craft.

"Hats off to honest merchants"

Materials

- Butcher paper
- Scissors
- Yarn
- Crayons or tempera paint
- Stapler

Directions

1. Divide into groups of four. Have each group select a different medieval craft to represent.

2. Cut butcher paper "aprons" for each member (see illustration). Staple yarn to tie the neck and waist.

3. The group members design an emblem and motto for their craft. (You may recreate the guild banners shown below on the chalkboard for student reference.)

4. Paint or color the guild design and motto on the apron. Make a group presentation with each member wearing their guild livery that describes their medieval craft.

Wheelmakers

Hatters

Candlemakers

Painters

Pastrymakers

Metalwork

Metals of all kinds were combined for many practical uses during the Middle Ages. A metalworker (or smith) worked to forge horseshoes, harnesses and stirrups. An armorer created the metal armor worn by knights. Nails of all sizes were everyday necessities. A metalworker also made thimbles for the seamstress and tools for the laborer. Lead was poured into molds to create figurines, plaques and badges. Individually cast keys locked everything from chests and caskets to castles. Castles had other metalwork needs including elaborate door hinges and barrel hoops. A heavy iron gate, called a *portcullis*, protected the castle entrance. Each diner in the great hall had a specially-made personal spoon.

Project

Design elaborate hinges for a medieval door.

Materials

- Aluminum foil
- Half-sheet brown construction paper
- Scissors
- Glue

Directions

1. Round the top of the construction paper to form an arched door.

2. Cut aluminum foil into elaborate shapes.

3. Glue the shapes to the door to resemble hinges.

Brass Portraits

Detailed engravings of knights in armor can sometimes be found in cathedrals and churches of the medieval period. These portraits were carefully engraved onto a sheet of metal very similar to brass. Skilled engravers showed accurate detail in their engravings. They were able to engrave each link in the knight's mesh mail, shield details and armor designs. Paint was sometimes applied to add color the the knight's flag or shield.

The portraits were usually made to honor an exemplary and famous knight who had died. The complete portraits were set in gravestones on the church floor or on top of raised tombs.

Project

Engrave a detailed portrait of a knight.

Materials

- Cardboard rectangle approximately 12 inches (30.48 cm) by 6 inches (15.24 cm) wide.
- Toothpicks
- Aluminum foil
- Clear tape
- Watercolor paints and brush
- Drawing paper, pencil

Directions

1. Cover the cardboard with aluminum foil. Tape the edges to the back side of the cardboard.

2. Sketch a knight on drawing paper cut to the same size as the cardboard.

3. Lay the drawing over the foil-covered cardboard. Use a toothpick to trace over the drawing. Press hard, but not so hard as to tear the paper.

4. Lift off the drawing paper. Use the toothpick again to carefully retrace any lines that did not imprint clearly.

5. Paint portions of the engraving with watercolors.

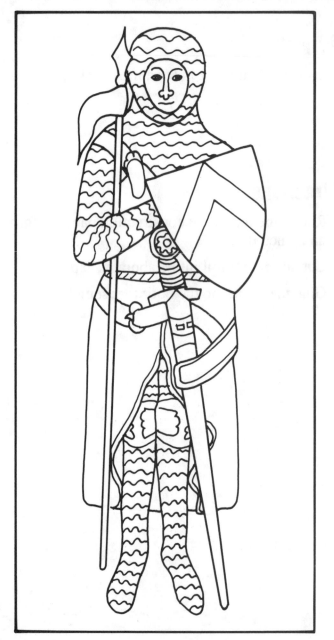

Dragons

Historical Aid

Dragons are mythical creatures found throughout stories and legends of medieval times. Legends describe them as large, lizard-like creatures that breathe fire and have a long, scaly tail. Some who lived during the Middle Ages blamed fire-breathing dragons for the destruction of crops, cities and other calamities. Dragons were also blamed for stealing jewels from the wealthy and cattle from nearby farms. According to medieval legends, dragons lived in wild, remote regions of the world and guarded stolen treasures in their dens. It was believed that a person who killed a dragon supposedly gained its wealth.

The dragon was also a popular heraldic symbol, found on shields and family crests.

Project

Combine the popular medieval art technique of pen and ink with crayon resist to paint a dragon.

Materials

- Black ink pens or thin black marking pens
- White construction paper
- Contrasting color construction paper
- Watercolor paints and brushes
- Crayons
- Scissors
- Glue

Directions

1. Use black pen to draw a picture of a dragon.

2. Color the picture heavily with crayon between the pen lines.

3. Paint a watercolor wash, the color of choice, over the entire paper.

4. When dry, cut out the dragon and glue it to a contrasting color construction paper.

5. As an extended activity, relate the dragon to a literature selection or write a new legend about a dragon that lived during medieval times.

Gargoyles

Historical Aid

The construction of a cathedral sometimes extended over two or three centuries. One generation planned it and another finished the work. Great lofty windows were filled with stained glass of exquisite colors. The Gothic arches of doorways and ceilings were ornamented with figures of saints and angels. The tops of pillars were carved with lace-like foliage.

On the roofs, stonecutters placed weird stone figures. Through the mouths of these figures rainwater from the roof drained. These carvings were called *gargoyles*, which means gullet (throat). They gained their name because of the gurgling noise the water made when passing through them. Gargoyles projected from the building as much as three feet (91 cm). Originally intended to protect the building from the effects of rain, the gargoyles became important decoration on medieval cathedrals.

Project

Make a milk carton gargoyle. Practice pouring water through its spout.

Materials

- Small milk carton, washed and dried
- Construction paper
- Tissue paper
- Aluminum foil
- Clear tape
- Glue
- Paper cup, water

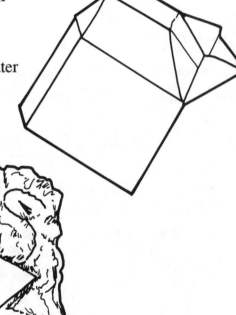

Directions

1. Open the milk carton spout. Cut a hole in the bottom of the milk carton at the opposite end.

2. Use a combination of aluminum foil, tissue paper and construction paper to wrap the milk carton and create a gargoyle.* (Keep the spout at the bottom.) Remember that a gargoyle was grotesque in appearance.

3. When the gargoyle is complete, pour water through the bottom and let it drain through the open spout. Discuss the purpose of the drainage.

Students may refer to historical pictures of medieval cathedrals to create more authentic gargoyles or they may create original designs based on information gained in the historical aid.